new interchange

English for international communication

Jack C. Richards

with Jonathan Hull and Susan Proctor

workbook

1B

New Interchange Workbook
revision prepared by Jonathan Hull.

CAMBRIDGE
UNIVERSITY PRESS

PUBLISHED BY THE PRESS SYNDICATE OF THE UNIVERSITY OF CAMBRIDGE
The Pitt Building, Trumpington Street, Cambridge, United Kingdom

CAMBRIDGE UNIVERSITY PRESS
The Edinburgh Building, Cambridge CB2 2RU, UK
40 West 20th Street, New York, NY 10011–4211, USA
477 Williamstown Road, Port Melbourne, VIC 3207, Australia
Ruiz de Alarcón 13, 28014 Madrid, Spain
Dock House, The Waterfront, Cape Town 8001, South Africa

http://www.cambridge.org

© Cambridge University Press 1997

This book is in copyright. Subject to statutory exception
and to the provisions of relevant collective licensing agreements,
no reproduction of any part may take place without
the written permission of Cambridge University Press.

First published 1997
10th printing 2002

New Interchange Workbook 1 has been developed from *Interchange* Workbook 1,
first published by Cambridge University Press in 1990.

Printed in Hong Kong, China

Typeface New Century Schoolbook   *System* QuarkXPress®   {AH}

A catalog record for this book is available from the British Library

ISBN 0 521 62881 4 Student's Book 1
ISBN 0 521 62880 6 Student's Book 1A
ISBN 0 521 62879 2 Student's Book 1B
ISBN 0 521 62878 4 Workbook 1
ISBN 0 521 62877 6 Workbook 1A
ISBN 0 521 62876 8 Workbook 1B
ISBN 0 521 62875 X Teacher's Edition 1
ISBN 0 521 62874 1 Teacher's Manual 1
ISBN 0 521 62873 3 Class Audio Cassettes 1
ISBN 0 521 62871 7 Student's Audio Cassette 1A
ISBN 0 521 62869 5 Student's Audio Cassette 1B
ISBN 0 521 62872 5 Class Audio CDs 1
ISBN 0 521 62870 9 Student's Audio CD 1A
ISBN 0 521 62868 7 Student's Audio CD 1B
ISBN 0 521 95019 8 Audio Sampler 1–3

Also available
ISBN 0 521 62867 9 Video 1 (NTSC)
ISBN 0 521 62866 0 Video 1 (PAL)
ISBN 0 521 62865 2 Video 1 (SECAM)
ISBN 0 521 62864 4 Video Activity Book 1
ISBN 0 521 62863 6 Video Teacher's Guide 1
ISBN 0 521 63887 9 Video Sampler 1–2
ISBN 0 521 62667 6 CD-ROM (PC format)
ISBN 0 521 62666 8 CD-ROM (Mac format)
ISBN 0 521 77381 4 Lab Guide 1
ISBN 0 521 77380 6 Lab Cassettes 1
ISBN 0 521 46759 4 Placement Test (valid for New
                   Interchange and Interchange)
ISBN 0 521 80575 9 Teacher-Training Video with
                   Video Manual
Forthcoming
ISBN 0 521 62882 2 New Interchange/Passages
                   Placement and Evaluation
                   Package

Book design, art direction, and layout services: Adventure House, NYC
Illustrators: Adventure House, Barbara Griffel, Randy Jones, Mark Kaufman, Kevin Spaulding, Sam Viviano
Photo researcher: Joan Scafarello

Contents

Acknowledgments

ILLUSTRATORS

Barbara Griffel 52 (*top*)
Randy Jones 49, 51, 52 (*bottom*)
Kevin Spaulding 5, 11, 13 (*top*), 23, 38, 48, 50, 53, 71
Sam Viviano 54, 60, 69, 70, 72, 76, 77, 90, 91, 92

PHOTOGRAPHIC CREDITS

The authors and publishers are grateful for permission to reproduce the following photographs. Every endeavor has been made to contact copyright owners, and apologies are expressed for omissions.

55 Photofest

56 (*clockwise from top left*) Blair Seitz/Photo Researchers; Richard Price/FPG; Thatcher Kalunzy/Tony Stone Images

57 (*upper left*) Doug Armand/Tony Stone Images; (*upper right*) Ken Straiton/The Stock Market; (*center left*) Ned Gillette/The Stock Market; (*center right*) Gary Landsman/The Stock Market; (*bottom left*) Jon Riley/Tony Stone Images; (*bottom right*) Viviane Moos/The Stock Market

59 (*from left to right*) Michael Goldman/FPG; Robert A. Isaacs/Photo Researchers; Hoa-Qui/Gamma Liaison; Frederick McKinney/FPG

61 (*top*) Will & Deni McIntyre/Tony Stone Images; (*bottom*) ZEFA, London/The Stock Market

62 (*left*) Richard Passmore/Tony Stone Images; (*center*) Guy Marche/FPG; (*right*) Superstock

63 Eric Sander/FPG

64 (*left*) Gavin Hellier/Tony Stone Images; (*center*) Jeffrey Sylvester/FPG; (*right*) Alexis Duclos/Gamma Liaison

65 Noboru Komine/Photo Researchers

74 (*top to bottom*) Matthew Klein/Photo Researchers; Peter Johansky/FPG; Roy Morsch/The Stock Market; Karen Leeds/The Stock Market; Alan Bergman/FPG

80 Travelpix/FPG

81 (*left*) Guido Alberto Rossi/The Image Bank; (*center*) Bob Abraham/Pacific Stock; (*right*) A & L Sinibaldi/Tony Stone Images

82 (*top*) Dennis Puleston/Photo Researchers; (*bottom*) Robert W. Hernandez/Photo Researchers

83 (*top to bottom*) Ken Fisher/Tony Stone Images; Telegraph Colour Library/FPG; Wolfgang Kaehler/Gamma Liaison; Karl Weidman/Photo Researchers; Donovan Reese/Tony Stone Images

93 (*left*) L.D. Gordon/The Image bank; (*center*) Ariel Skelley/The Stock Market; (*right*) John Henly/The Stock Market

94 Superstock

9 What does he look like?

1

Write the opposites. Use the words in the box.

| ☐ light | ☑ straight | ☐ young | ☐ short | ☐ tall |

1. curly / *straight*_____

2. dark / _____

3. elderly / _____

4. long / _____

5. short / _____

2 *Collocations*

A Match the words in columns A and B to make descriptions.
Write the descriptions.

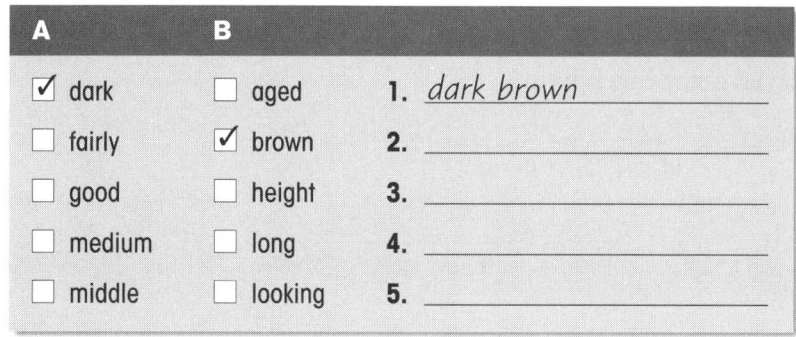

A	B	
☑ dark	☐ aged	**1.** *dark brown*_____
☐ fairly	☑ brown	**2.** _____
☐ good	☐ height	**3.** _____
☐ medium	☐ long	**4.** _____
☐ middle	☐ looking	**5.** _____

B Answer the questions using the descriptions from part A.

1. A: What does he look like?

   B: *He's good-looking.*_____

2. A: How long is his hair?

   B: _____

3. A: What color is his hair?

   B: _____

4. A: How old is he?

   B: _____

5. A: How tall is he?

   B: _____

3 *Complete the conversation with questions.*

Jim: *What does she look like?*

Steve: She's quite pretty, with straight black hair.

Jim: And _____

Steve: It's medium length.

Jim: _____

Steve: She's fairly tall.

Jim: And _____

Steve: She's in her early twenties.

Jim: _____

Steve: Sometimes. I think she's wearing them now.

Jim: OK. I think I see her over there.

4 *Describe yourself. How old are you? What do you look like?*
What are you wearing today?

_____

_____

_____

_____

_____

_____

5 Circle two things in each description that do not match the picture. Then correct the information.

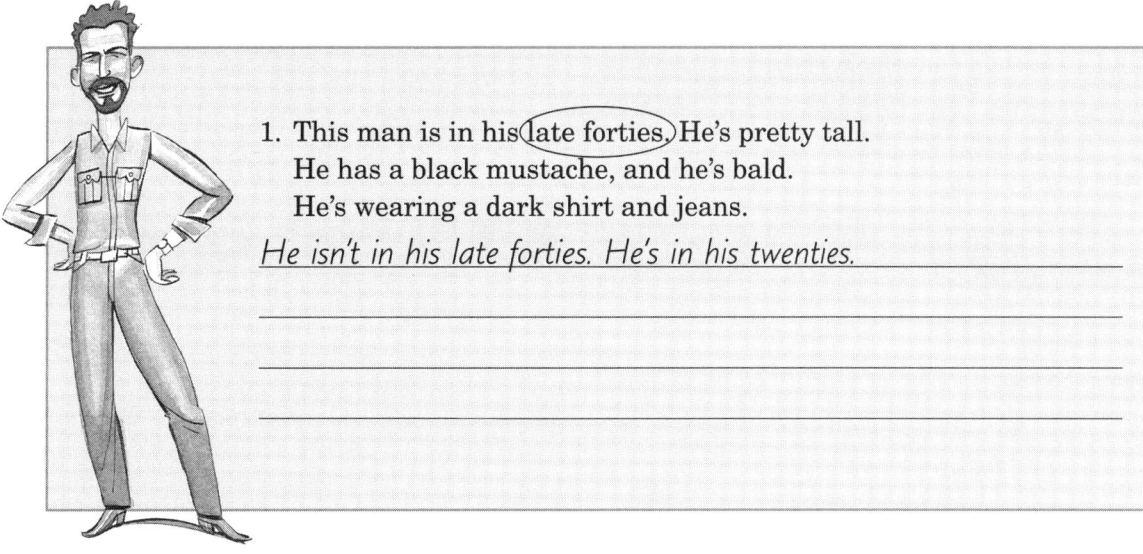

1. This man is in his (late forties.) He's pretty tall.
   He has a black mustache, and he's bald.
   He's wearing a dark shirt and jeans.

   He isn't in his late forties. He's in his twenties.

   _____

   _____

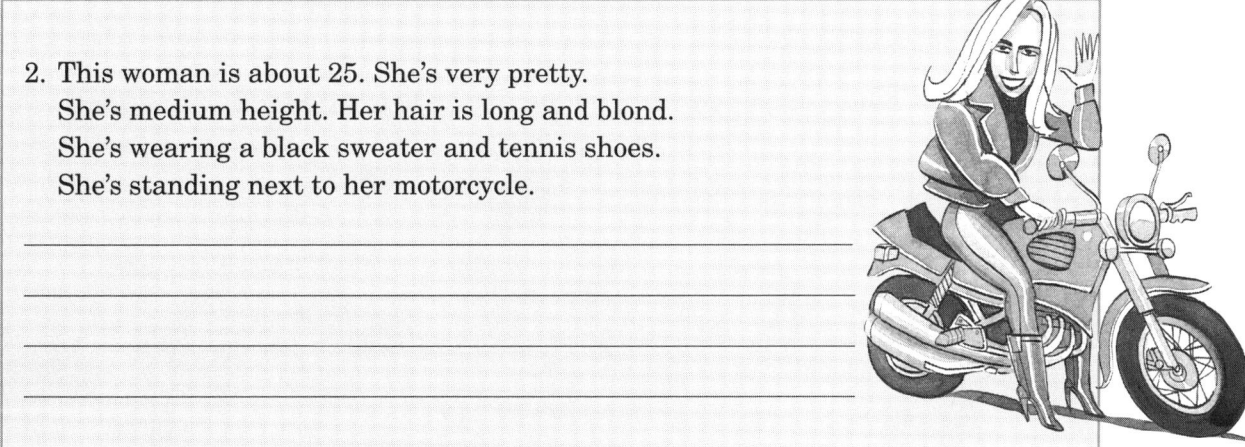

2. This woman is about 25. She's very pretty.
   She's medium height. Her hair is long and blond.
   She's wearing a black sweater and tennis shoes.
   She's standing next to her motorcycle.

   _____

   _____

   _____

   _____

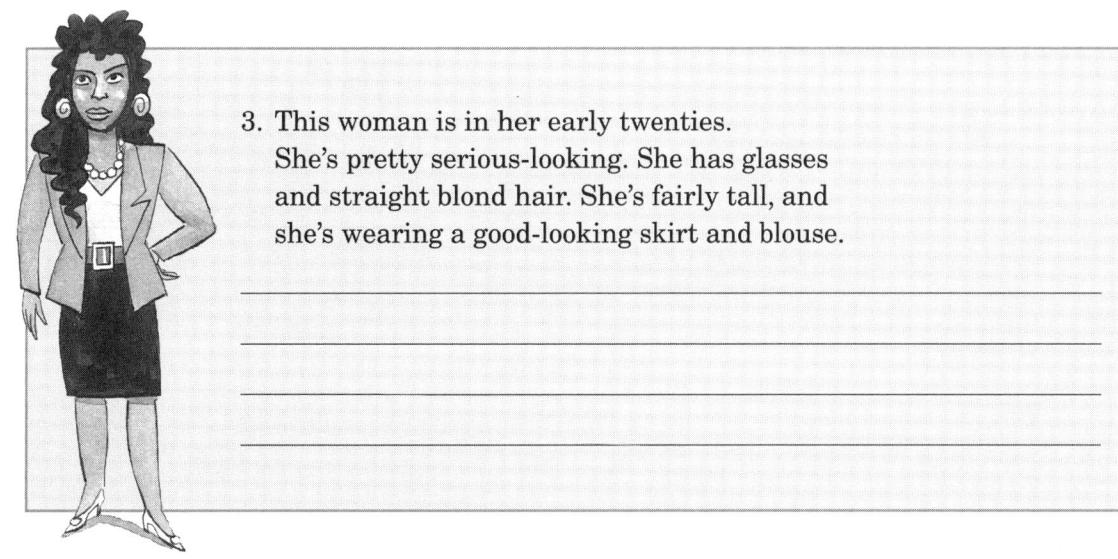

3. This woman is in her early twenties.
   She's pretty serious-looking. She has glasses
   and straight blond hair. She's fairly tall, and
   she's wearing a good-looking skirt and blouse.

   _____

   _____

   _____

   _____

6 *Which clothing items are more formal? Which are more informal or casual? Use words from the list. Complete the chart.*

☑ blouse	☐ shorts	☐ skirt
☐ boots	☐ running shoes	☐ suit
☐ dress	☐ scarf	☐ tie
☐ jeans	☐ T-shirt	☐ cap

Formal	Casual
blouse	

7 *Write a sentence about each person. Use the words in the box and participles.*

Mandy

Edward and Kate

William

Giorgio

Alice

☑ man	☐ carry a jacket
☐ woman	☐ wear sunglasses
☐ one	☐ stand next to Alice
☐ ones	☐ talk to the man
☐ tall woman	☑ wear a suit and tie

1. *William is the man wearing a suit and tie.*

2. _____

3. _____

4. _____

5. _____

8 *Answer the questions. Use the words given.*

1. A: Which one is Marie?

   B: *She's the one in the gray dress.* _____ (gray dress)

2. A: Which one is Carlos?

   B: _____ (couch)

3. A: Which ones are Dan and Cindy?

   B: _____ (Marie)

4. A: Which one is Angela?

   B: _____ (couch)

5. A: Who's Kim?

   B: _____ (short black hair)

9 *Rewrite these sentences and questions.*
Find another way to say them using the words given.

1. A: Who's Mika?

   Which one's Mika? _____ (Which)

   B: She's the one in the black dress.

   She's the one wearing the black dress. _____ (wearing)

2. A: Which ones are the teachers?

   _____ (Who)

   B: They're the ones on the couch.

   _____ (sitting)

3. A: Which one is Larry?

   _____ (Who)

   B: He's the guy wearing the coat.

   _____ (in)

10 Complete this description. Use the present continuous or the participle of the verbs in the box.

☐ ask   ☐ carry   ☑ look   ☐ stand   ☐ talk   ☐ wait   ☐ walk   ☐ wear

Yeah, it's really quiet.
Nothing ever really happens here . . . .
I'_m looking_____ out my window . . . . Let's see . . . .
There's a good-looking middle-aged woman _____
her dog, and a young guy _____ on the phone. Two people
_____ next to him. Hey! The one _____ a
baseball hat is my classmate! Some people _____ at the
bus stop. A serious-looking woman _____ for directions.
And hey, here comes a really cute woman _____ a
backpack. Wait a minute! I know her. That's my
old girlfriend. I have to go now! Bye.

DORMITORY

BUS STOP M5

TELEPHONE

11 Choose the correct responses.

1. A: Where's Jan?

   B: _She couldn't make it._____
   - ■ I'd like to meet her.
   - ■ She couldn't make it.

2. A: Who's Sam?

   B: _____
   - ■ I'm afraid I missed him.
   - ■ The handsome guy near the door.

3. A: Is she the one on the couch?

   B: _____
   - ■ That's right.
   - ■ Let's see.

4. A: How tall is she?

   B: _____
   - ■ Fairly long.
   - ■ Pretty short.

10 Have you ever ridden a camel?

1 *Match the verb forms in columns A and B.*

A	B
1. be __d__	a. gone
2. call _____	b. done
3. do _____	c. seen
4. eat _____	✓ d. been
5. go _____	e. called
6. have _____	f. jogged
7. jog _____	g. made
8. make _____	h. had
9. see _____	i. tried
10. try _____	j. eaten

2 *Complete the questions in these conversations.*
Use the present perfect of the verbs in Exercise 1.

1. A: *Have you seen* _____ the new Keanu Reeves movie?

   B: Yes, it's very good.

2. A: _____ running lately?

   B: Yes, she usually runs in the morning and evening.

3. A: _____ at the new Brazilian restaurant?

   B: Yes, we've already eaten there. It's excellent, but very expensive.

4. A: How many times _____

   shopping at the mall this month?

   B: Actually, I haven't gone at all. Let's go today! I hear

   there's a new music store there.

5. A: How many international phone calls

   _____ this week?

   B: Only one – on my father's birthday.

Keanu Reeves

3 Already *and* yet

A Check (✓) the things you've done. Put an ✗ next to the things you haven't done.

1. _____ gone in-line skating
2. _____ stayed up all night
3. _____ been to a jazz club
4. _____ had a part-time job
5. _____ tried skiing
6. _____ gotten married
7. _____ made friends in class
8. _____ seen a rock concert

getting married

skiing

in-line skating

B Look at the things you checked and marked ✗ in part A. Write sentences about them. Use *already* and *yet*.

> **Grammar note: Already *and* yet**
>
> ***Already*** **is used in positive statements with the present perfect.**
> I've **already** gone in-line skating.
> ***Yet*** **is used in negative statements with the present perfect.**
> I haven't gone in-line skating **yet**.

1. _____
2. _____
3. _____
4. _____
5. _____
6. _____
7. _____
8. _____

4 *Look at the pictures. How often have you done these things?*
Write sentences using the expressions in the box.

I've often	I've . . . once or twice.
I've . . . three or four times.	I haven't . . . lately.
I've . . . several times.	I've never . . . .

ride a roller coaster

go to a nightclub

1. _____

4. _____

go bungee jumping

call home

2. _____

5. _____

see an opera

play tennis

3. _____

6. _____

5 *Horror stories!*

A Have you ever had a terrible day? What happened? What went wrong?

B Read these stories.

NO WAY UP!

Have you ever been in a cable car? Well, I have. Last February, I went on a ski trip to Switzerland. What a trip! The first morning, I got into a cable car. I wanted to go to the top of the mountain and ski down. The cable car started up the mountain. I looked down, and it was so beautiful. Then there was a terrible noise. Suddenly the car stopped. It didn't move, and there was quiet everywhere.

It was cold, and it began to get dark and snow. I was alone for one hour, two hours. I thought, "They've forgotten me!" At last the car started back down the mountain. It went very fast. "Sorry," a man said when I climbed out of the car. "We've never had this problem before. Please, try again tomorrow." "He's joking," I thought. "I've had enough of cable cars for a lifetime."

NO WAY OUT!

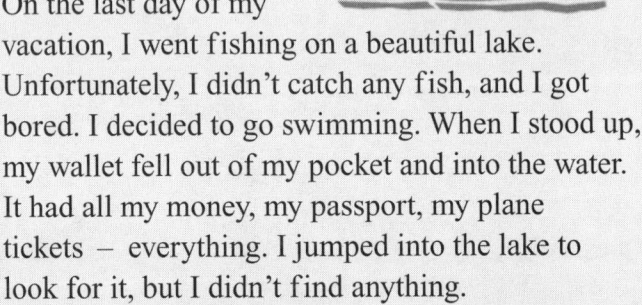

I have always wanted to go fishing. Last summer, I went on a trip to Taiwan. On the last day of my vacation, I went fishing on a beautiful lake. Unfortunately, I didn't catch any fish, and I got bored. I decided to go swimming. When I stood up, my wallet fell out of my pocket and into the water. It had all my money, my passport, my plane tickets – everything. I jumped into the lake to look for it, but I didn't find anything.

The next morning, I wasn't able to leave the hotel. I had no money to pay the bill and no plane ticket or passport to go home. So what did I do? I called my boss and asked for some money. I have never had such a terrible experience.

C In which story or stories did the writer(s) do these things?
Write *1*, *2*, or *1 and 2*.

____1____ stayed in the mountains

_____ lost a wallet

_____ enjoyed the view

_____ got no exercise

_____ spent time on a boat

_____ waited for help

_____ went swimming

_____ had a terrible day

6 *Look at the answers. Write questions using* **Have you ever . . . ?**

flamenco dancing

sumo wrestlers

oysters

wall climbing

1. A: *Have you ever watched flamenco dancing?*
   B: Yes, I have. I watched flamenco dancing last summer in Spain.

2. A: _____
   B: Actually, I saw a sumo wrestling match last month on TV. It was terrific.

3. A: _____
   B: No, I haven't. I've never been camping.

4. A: _____
   B: Yes, I have. I ate oysters last year in France.

5. A: _____
   B: Yes, I went wall climbing on Friday night.

6. A: _____
   B: Yes, I have. My brother once let me ride his motorcycle.

7. A: _____
   B: No, I've never been to India.

8. A: _____
   B: Yes, I had a bad dream just last night.

---

7 *Write your own answers to the questions in Exercise 6.*
Use expressions like the ones from the list.

Yes, I have. I . . . yesterday.	No, I haven't. I've never . . . .
I . . . on Monday.	
I . . . last year.	
I . . . in August.	

1. _____
2. _____
3. _____
4. _____
5. _____
6. _____
7. _____
8. _____

8 Complete the conversation. Use the past tense or the present perfect of the words given.

A: ___Have___ you ever ___lost___ (lose) anything valuable?

B: Yes, I _____ (lose) my watch last month.

A: _____ you _____ (find) it yet?

B: No. Actually, I _____ already _____ (buy) a new one. Look!

A: Oh, that's nice. Where _____ you _____ (buy) it?

B: I _____ (get) it at the street market last weekend. What about

you? _____ you ever _____ (lose) anything valuable?

A: Well, I _____ (leave) my address book in a pay phone a couple

of months ago.

B: How annoying! Maybe that's why you _____ (not call)

me for a while.

A: That's right. I can't even remember my own phone number! But you

_____ (not call) me in a long time. What's your excuse?

B: I told you. I _____ (lose) my watch, so I

_____ (not have) the time!

A: Very funny!

I haven't had the time.

9 Choose the correct responses.

1. A: Has she called her family lately?

   B: _No, she hasn't._____
   - How many times?
   - No, she hasn't.

2. A: Are you having a good time?

   B: _____
   - In a long time.
   - Really good.

3. A: How many times has he seen the show?

   B: _____
   - Twice.
   - Already.

4. A: What about a tour of the city?

   B: _____
   - I've never, have you?
   - Sure. I hear it's great.

11 It's a very exciting city!

1 *Choose the correct words to complete the sentences.*

New York City

Rome, Italy

1. Prices are very high in New York City. Everything is pretty _____*expensive*_____ there. (cheap/expensive/stressful)

2. My hometown is not an exciting place. The nightlife there is pretty _____. (boring/nice/interesting)

3. Rome is a beautiful old city. There are not many _____ buildings.   (big/modern/small)

4. Some parts of this city are fairly dangerous. They're not very _____ late at night. (hot/interesting/safe)

5. Athens is a very quiet city in the winter. The streets are never _____ at that time of the year. (clean/crowded/relaxing)

2 *Choose the correct questions to complete this conversation.*

☐ What's the weather like?
☐ Is it big?
☐ Is the nightlife exciting?
☐ What's your hometown like?

A: _____

B: My hometown? Oh, it's a pretty nice place.

A: _____

B: No, it's fairly small, and it has a lot of beautiful buildings.

A: _____

B: The winter is wet and too cold. It's very nice in the summer, though.

A: _____

B: No! It's really boring after six o'clock in the evening.

3 *Choose the correct conjunctions and rewrite the sentences.*

> **Language note:** and, but, however, *and* though
>
> **Use *and* for additional information.**
> It's an exciting city, **and** the weather is great.
>
> **Use *but*, *however*, and *though* for contrasting information.**
> It's very safe in the day, **but** it's pretty dangerous at night.
> It is a fairly large city. It's not too interesting, **however**.
> The summers are hot. The evenings are fairly cold, **though**.

Paris, France

Prague, the Czech Republic

A hometown in the U.S.

1. Paris is a very busy place. The streets are always crowded.   (and/but)

   Paris is a very busy place, and the streets are always crowded.

   _____

2. Prague is a very nice place. The winters are terribly cold.   (and/though)

   _____

   _____

3. Sydney is a relaxing city. It has a wonderful harbor.   (and/however)

   _____

   _____

4. My hometown is a great place for a vacation. It's not too good for shopping.
   (and/but)

   _____

   _____

5. Our hometown is fairly ugly and dirty. It has some beautiful old houses.
   (and/however)

   _____

   _____

4 *Check (✓) if these sentences need* a *or* an. *Then write* a *or* an *in the correct places.*

> ### Grammar note: a *and* an
>
> **Use** *a* **or** *an* **with (adverb +) adjective + singular noun.**
> It has **a fairly new park.**
> It's **an old city.**
>
> **Don't use** *a* **or** *an* **with (adverb +) adjective.**
> It's not **very old.**
> It's **dirty.**

Denver International Airport

1. ☑ Denver has _∧*a* very modern airport.
2. ☐ Restaurants are very cheap in Mexico.
3. ☐ Copenhagen is clean city.
4. ☐ The buildings in Paris are really beautiful.
5. ☐ Apartments are very expensive in Hong Kong.
6. ☐ Amsterdam is fairly crowded city in the summer.
7. ☐ Toronto has good museums.
8. ☐ Rio is exciting place to visit.

5 *Complete this description of London with* **is** *or* **has.**

TRAVEL BRITAIN

London ____is____ Britain's biggest city. It _____ a very old capital and dates back to the Romans. It _____ a city of interesting buildings and churches, and it _____ many beautiful parks. It also _____ some of the best museums in the world. London _____ very crowded in the summer, but it _____ not too busy in the winter. It _____ a popular city with foreign tourists and _____ more than eight million visitors a year. The city _____ famous for its shopping and _____ many excellent department stores. London _____ convenient trains and buses that cross the city, so it _____ easy for tourists to get around.

6 *From city to city*

A Read about these cities.

Budapest

For many centuries, Budapest was two cities, with Buda on the west side of the river Danube and Pest on the east side. Budapest became one city in 1872, and it has been the capital city of Hungary for about eighty years.

The population of Budapest is about three million, and the city is a very popular place for tourists. Visitors like to take boat rides along the Danube. Budapest is also known for its exciting nightlife. The best time to visit is the summer since Budapest is very cold in the winter.

Los Angeles

Los Angeles was founded in 1781. With 3.5 million people, it is now the biggest city in California and the second largest city in the United States. It is famous for its modern freeways, its movie stars, and its smog. When the city is really smoggy, you can't see the nearby mountains. The weather is usually dry and warm. Visitors like to go to the film studios and to drive along Hollywood Boulevard. There are some good beaches near the city, and Los Angeles is also close to Disneyland.

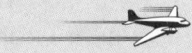

Taipei

Since the founding of Taipei in the eighteenth century, the city has grown to a population of 2.3 million and has become the cultural, industrial, and administrative center of the island of Taiwan. Taipei is an exciting city, but the weather is humid and not always pleasant.

It's also a very busy city, and the streets are always full of people. There is an excellent museum that many tourists visit. Taipei is a fairly expensive city, but not more expensive than some neighboring cities such as Hong Kong and Tokyo. So more and more tourists go to Taipei to shop.

B Complete the chart.

City	Date founded	Population	Weather	Tourist attractions
Budapest	*1872*	*3 million*		
Los Angeles				
Taipei				

C Complete the sentences.

1. *Taipei* _____ is cheaper than other cities nearby.
2. _____ has good beaches nearby.
3. _____ was once two cities.
4. _____ were both founded in the eighteenth century.

7 *Complete the sentences. Use words from the list.*

☐ shouldn't miss	☐ can take
☑ should see	☐ shouldn't stay
☐ should travel	☐ shouldn't walk

1. You _should see_ the new zoo.
   It's very interesting.

2. You _____ near the
   airport. It's too noisy.

3. You _____ the museum.
   It has some new exhibits.

4. You _____ a bus tour
   of the city if you like.

5. You _____ alone at
   night. It's too dangerous.

6. You _____ by taxi if
   you're out late.

8 *Complete this conversation with should or shouldn't and I or you.*

A: I'm taking my vacation in Indonesia.
   What _____should I_____ do there?

B: _____ miss Jogjakarta,
   the old capital city. There are a lot of
   beautiful old buildings. For example,
   _____ see the
   temple of Borobudur.

A: Sounds great. Bali is very popular, too.
   _____ go there?

B: Yes, _____ .
   It's very interesting.

A: _____ take a lot of
   money with me?

B: No, _____ . Indonesia
   is not an expensive country.

A: So when _____
   go there?

B: Well, it's always hot and humid,
   so it really doesn't matter.

Jogjakarta, Indonesia

9 **Ask questions about a place you want to visit.**
Use can, should, *or* shouldn't. *Ask about:*

1. the time to visit
   What time of year should you visit?

2. things to see and do there

3. things people shouldn't do

4. special foods

5. things to buy

6. other interesting things

10 *Rewrite these sentences. Find another way to say each sentence*
using the words given.

1. It's a stressful city.
   It isn't a relaxing city.   (not relaxing)

2. The streets are always full of people.
   _____   (crowded)

3. It's not a very beautiful city.
   _____   (fairly ugly)

4. When should we visit the city?
   _____   (a good time)

5. You really should see the flea markets.
   _____   (not miss)

6. What can we do there?
   _____   (should)

12 It really works!

1 *Any suggestions?*

A Check (✓) the best advice for each health problem.

1. a backache
- ✓ use a heating pad
- ☐ get some exercise
- ☐ take some vitamin C

2. a headache
- ☐ take some vitamin C
- ☐ take some aspirin
- ☐ take some good advice

3. a bad cold
- ☐ see a dentist
- ☐ go to bed and rest
- ☐ take some good advice

4. an insect bite
- ☐ put anti-itch cream on it
- ☐ take some aspirin
- ☐ drink lots of liquids

5. the hiccups
- ☐ drink lots of hot water
- ☐ take some cold medicine
- ☐ chop up some garlic

B Write a question about each problem in part A. Then write answers using the words from the list. Use the ideas in part A or your own suggestions in your answers.

It's important	It's helpful . . . .
It's a good idea	It's useful . . . .

1. A: *What should you do for a backache?*
   B: *It's helpful to use a heating pad.*

2. A: _____
   B: _____

3. A: _____
   B: _____

4. A: _____
   B: _____

5. A: _____
   B: _____

2 Rewrite these sentences. Find another way to give advice using It's a good idea . . . , It's helpful . . . , or It's important . . . .

Language note: Negative infinitive complements		
Problem	**Advice**	**Negative infinitive advice**
For the flu,	don't exercise a lot.	For the flu, it's a good idea **not to exercise** a lot.

1. For a bad cough, don't smoke.

   For a bad cough, it's important not to smoke.

2. For a sore throat, don't talk too much.

   _____

3. For a burn, don't put ice on it.

   _____

4. For insomnia, don't drink coffee at night.

   _____

5. For a fever, don't get out of bed.

   _____

3 Check (✓) three health problems you have had this year. Write what you did for each one. Use the remedies below or your own remedies.

Health problems

☐ a backache
☐ a headache
☐ a toothache
☐ a cold
☐ a sore throat
☐ the hiccups
☐ a sunburn
☐ stress

Some remedies

take some aspirin   get some medicine from the drugstore
use some lotion   put some ointment on it
take some cough drops   see my doctor/dentist
go to bed   do nothing

Example: *Yesterday, I had a bad headache so I took some aspirin.*

1. _____
2. _____
3. _____

4 Getting to sleep

A How many hours do you sleep each night? Do you ever have difficulty getting to sleep? What do you do? Read the article.

Sleep

Most people need seven to eight hours of sleep a night. Some people need less than this, and some people need more.

According to sleep expert Dr. Robert Schachter, many people have difficulty sleeping, but they do not know why. Most people know it is important not to drink coffee or tea before they go to bed – both beverages have caffeine. Caffeine keeps people awake. However, not everybody knows that some medicines, such as cold tablets, also have caffeine in them. Stress can cause insomnia, too. Busy people with stressful jobs may not be able to sleep at night.

Dr. Schachter suggests, "You shouldn't use your bedroom as a TV room or an exercise room. You should use it for sleeping only. It's a good idea to have a regular sleeping schedule. Get up and go to bed at the same time every day. It's also important not to eat before bedtime. Eating may keep you awake."

And if all this doesn't work, try counting sheep!

B Check (✓) True or False.

	True	False
1. Everyone needs eight hours of sleep a night.	☐	☐
2. Caffeine helps you fall asleep.	☐	☐
3. Cold tablets can keep you awake.	☐	☐
4. Busy people may have trouble falling asleep.	☐	☐
5. It is a good idea to have a TV near your bed.	☐	☐
6. You should have regular sleeping hours.	☐	☐
7. You shouldn't eat just before you go to bed.	☐	☐
8. Counting sheep may help.	☐	☐

5 *What do you suggest?*

A Complete the word map with medicines from the list.

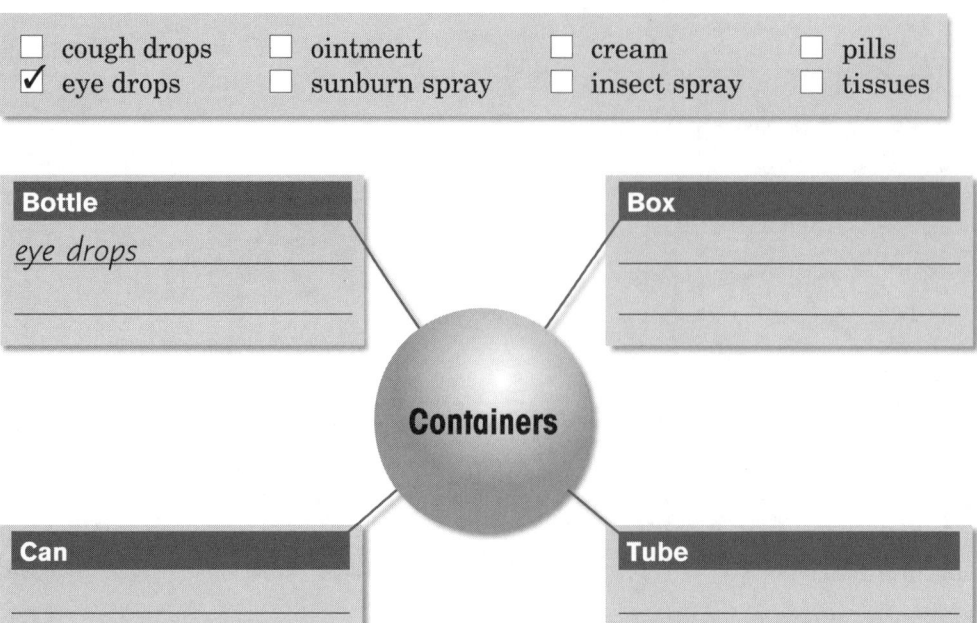

☐ cough drops	☐ ointment	☐ cream	☐ pills
☑ eye drops	☐ sunburn spray	☐ insect spray	☐ tissues

Bottle
eye drops
_____

Box
_____
_____

Containers

Can
_____
_____

Tube
_____
_____

B What should these people buy? Give advice. Use the containers and medicine from part A.

1. Joe has very tired eyes.

   He should buy a bottle of eye drops.

2. Mary has a bad cold.

   _____

3. Andrew and Carlos have a lot of insect bites.

   _____

4. David has dry skin.

   _____

6 Check (✓) the correct sentences to make conversations.

I'm here to help

1. Pharmacist: ☑ Can I help you?
   ☐ Should I help you?

   Customer: ☐ Yes. Can I have a package of bandages?
   ☐ Yes. I suggest a package of bandages.

   Pharmacist: Here you are.

   Customer: ☐ And what do you need for a sunburn?
   ☐ And what do you have for a sunburn?

   Pharmacist: ☐ Do you suggest this lotion?
   ☐ I suggest this lotion.

   Customer: Thanks.

2. Pharmacist: Hi. Can I help you?

   Customer: ☐ Yes. Can I suggest something for sore muscles?
   ☐ Yes. Could I have something for sore muscles?

   Pharmacist: ☐ Sure. Try this ointment.
   ☐ Sure. Could I try this ointment?

   Customer: ☐ Thanks. And what should you get for the flu?
   ☐ Thanks. And what do you suggest for the flu?

   Pharmacist: ☐ Can I have some of these tablets? They really work.
   ☐ Try some of these tablets. They really work.

   Customer: ☐ OK, thanks. I'll take them. And you should get a box of tissues.
   ☐ OK, thanks. I'll take them. And could I have a box of tissues?

   Pharmacist: Sure. Here you are.

7 *Complete this conversation with the correct words.*

A: Wow, you don't look very good! Do you feel OK?

B: No, I think I'm getting a cold. What should I do _____ it?
(for/to/with)

A: You should stay _____ home and go _____ bed.
(at/in/of)   (in/of/to)

B: You're probably right. I've got a really bad cough, too.

A: Try drinking some hot tea _____ honey. It really helps.
(for/of/with)

B: Anything else?

A: Yeah, I suggest you get a big box _____ tissues!
(at/in/of)

8 *Give suggestions for these problems. Use words from the box.*

I suggest	You should	Try . . . .

1. I have a very sore throat.

   Try some hot tea.

2. I think I'm getting a cold.

   _____

3. I have a backache. And don't tell me to go to bed!

   _____

4. I have a terrible stomachache.

   _____

13 May I take your order, please?

1 *Show that you agree. Write sentences with the words given.*

I don't want fast food tonight.

I really like healthy foods.

1. *I don't either.* _____ (either)

2. _____ (so)

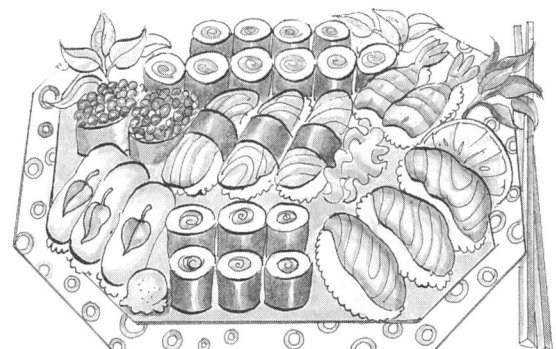

I'm in the mood for Japanese food.

I don't like spicy food.

3. _____ (too)

4. _____ (neither)

I don't like bland food very much.

I think Italian food is delicious.

5. _____ (either)

6. _____ (too)

2 *What do you think?*

A Look at the pictures. Write sentences about the food.
Use the expressions in the box.

Useful expressions

I like . . . a lot.   I don't like . . . very much.
I love . . . .   I'm not crazy about . . . .
I'm crazy about . . . .   It's a bit too . . . .
I can't stand . . . .

 greasy

1. *It's a bit too greasy.*

 healthy

2. _____

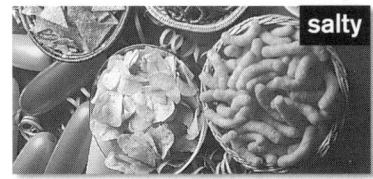 salty

3. _____

 bland

4. _____

 rich

5. _____

 Japanese

6. _____

B List your two favorite kinds of food.

_____

_____

3 *Which restaurant?*

A What kinds of restaurants do you like?
Do you prefer a quiet place or a noisy place?

B Read these restaurant reviews.

★★★★

Trattoria Romana is an excellent Italian restaurant. It has a quiet and relaxing atmosphere, and the service is very good. It's always crowded, so make a reservation early. The menu is not very big. There are only four entrees on the menu, but everything is fresh. The chicken with pasta is wonderful. Desserts are their specialty – rich and delicious! It's a little expensive but very good. You'll spend about $25 per person.

★★

Last Saturday, I was the only customer at ***Dynasty***, a new diner on 57th Street. It's not a good place to go. The waiters are slow and unfriendly. The atmosphere is boring, and so is the menu. It specializes in American food – mostly steak and potatoes; but my steak was raw, and the fries were greasy. It isn't cheap, either. It cost me $22. If you go to Dynasty, you certainly won't need a reservation. My advice, however, is "Don't Go."

★★★

Beirut Cafe is a great new Lebanese restaurant. The specialty is *meze* – lots of different small dishes, some with meat or fish, others with vegetables. The atmosphere is lively, and the service is very friendly. There's live Lebanese music and dancing on weekends. Beirut Cafe is surprisingly inexpensive – about $18 a person, but you need to make a reservation.

C Complete the chart.

	Trattoria Romana	Dynasty	Beirut Cafe
Food	*Italian*		
Atmosphere	*quiet and relaxing*		
Specialties			
Service			
Price/person			
Reservation	☐ yes ☐ no	☐ yes ☐ no	☐ yes ☐ no

4 *Create a menu. Use words from the box.*

☐ beef	☐ clam	☐ milk	☐ onion	☑ salmon
☐ cake	☐ coffee	☐ mixed	☐ pasta	☐ sandwich
☐ chicken	☐ ice	☐ noodle	☐ pie	☐ tea

★ ★ Kate's Diner ★ ★

★ Main Dishes ★
(includes salad and choice of potatoes)

grilled *salmon* _____

roast _____

turkey _____

★ Salads ★

_____ salad

_____ salad

_____ greens

★ Soups ★

chicken _____ soup

French _____ soup

_____ chowder

★ Desserts ★

chocolate _____

apple _____

_____ cream

★ Beverages ★

_____   _____   _____

---

5 *Use one or more words to complete this conversation between a waiter and a customer.*

Waiter: May I take your order?

Customer: *Yes, I'll have* _____ the roast beef with mashed potatoes.

Waiter: What kind of dressing _____ on your salad – French, Italian or vinaigrette?

Customer: French, _____ .

Waiter: And would you like _____ to drink?

Customer: Yes, _____ have iced coffee.

Waiter: Anything else?

Customer: No, _____ .

6 *Choose the correct responses.*

1. A: Would you like fries or cole slaw?

   B: *I'll have the cole slaw, please.*
   - I guess I will, thanks.
   - I'll have the cole slaw, please.
   - Yes, please.

2. A: What kind of soda would you like?

   B: _____
   - I'll have a cola.
   - I'd like a hot dog, please.
   - A small order, please.

3. A: Would you like anything to drink?

   B: _____
   - No, thanks.
   - Yes, a hamburger, please.
   - I'll have chocolate cake, please.

4. A: What flavor ice cream would you like?

   B: _____
   - Baked, please.
   - Vanilla, please.
   - Ice cream, please.

5. A: Would you like anything else?

   B: _____
   - Yes, thank you very much.
   - Not at all, thanks.
   - That will be all, thanks.

7 Complete the conversation. Use the words and expressions in the box.

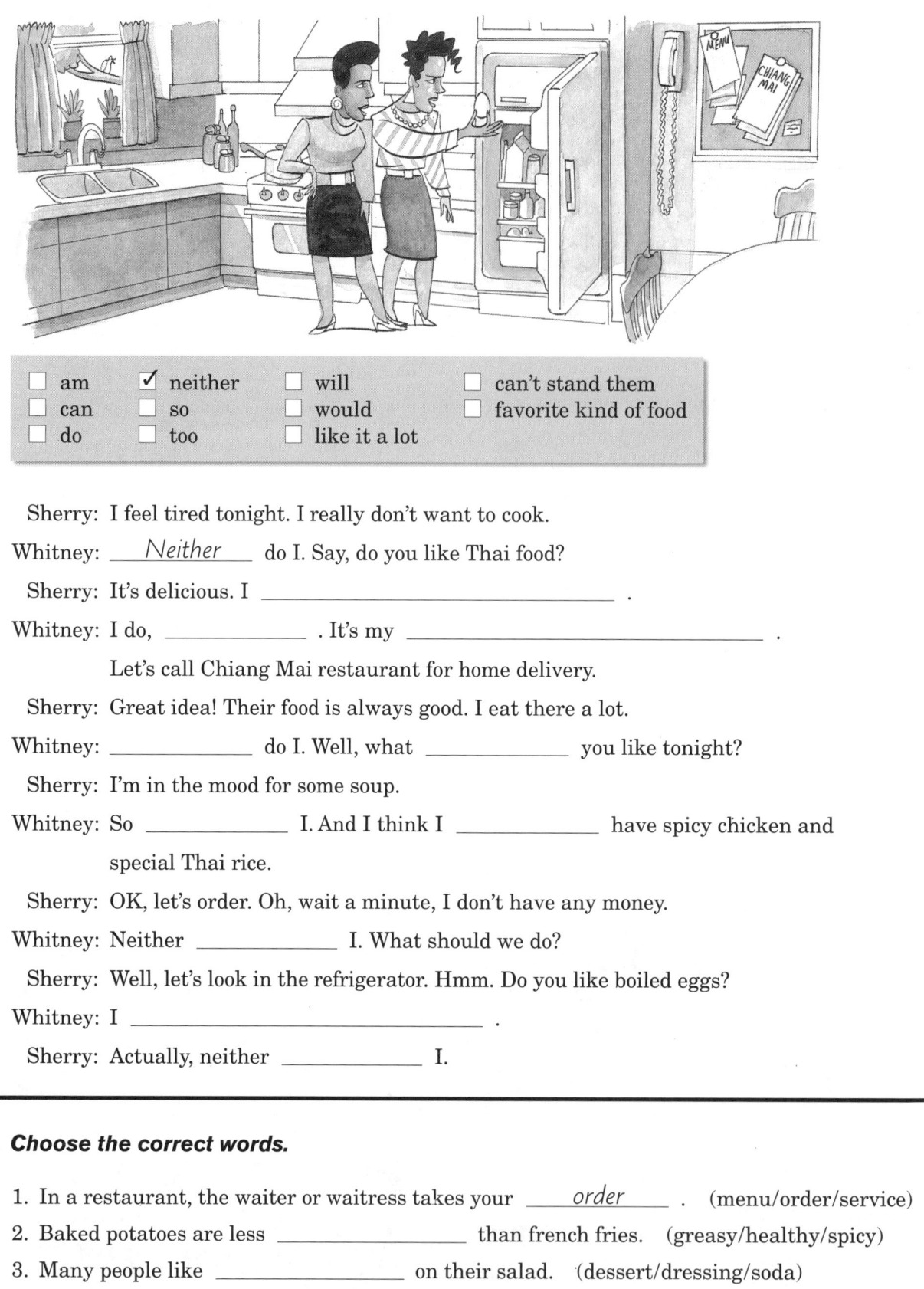

☐ am	✓ neither	☐ will	☐ can't stand them
☐ can	☐ so	☐ would	☐ favorite kind of food
☐ do	☐ too	☐ like it a lot	

Sherry: I feel tired tonight. I really don't want to cook.

Whitney: _____Neither_____ do I. Say, do you like Thai food?

Sherry: It's delicious. I _____ .

Whitney: I do, _____ . It's my _____ .

Let's call Chiang Mai restaurant for home delivery.

Sherry: Great idea! Their food is always good. I eat there a lot.

Whitney: _____ do I. Well, what _____ you like tonight?

Sherry: I'm in the mood for some soup.

Whitney: So _____ I. And I think I _____ have spicy chicken and

special Thai rice.

Sherry: OK, let's order. Oh, wait a minute, I don't have any money.

Whitney: Neither _____ I. What should we do?

Sherry: Well, let's look in the refrigerator. Hmm. Do you like boiled eggs?

Whitney: I _____ .

Sherry: Actually, neither _____ I.

8 Choose the correct words.

1. In a restaurant, the waiter or waitress takes your _____order_____ . (menu/order/service)

2. Baked potatoes are less _____ than french fries. (greasy/healthy/spicy)

3. Many people like _____ on their salad. (dessert/dressing/soda)

4. Some people rarely cook with spices. They prefer _____ food. (bland/hot/rich)

5. Vanilla is a popular ice cream _____ . (drink/flavor/meal)

14 The biggest and the best!

1 Geography

A Circle the correct word.

1. This is an area of land between two rows of mountains or cliffs, usually with a river running through.
   (a.) canyon   b. plain   c. waterfall

2. This is a large area of land that has lots of trees on it.
   a. cliff   b. forest   c. valley

3. This is an area of land that is always wet.
   a. canyon   b. plain   c. swamp

4. This is an area of water with land all around it.
   a. lake   b. ocean   c. swamp

5. This is a mountain with a hole at the top. Smoke and lava sometimes come from the hole, and it can be dangerous.
   a. hill   b. plateau   c. volcano

6. This is a dry, sandy place. It doesn't rain much here, and there aren't many plants.
   a. desert   b. sea   c. volcano

B Complete the names. Use words from the box.

☑ Canyon	☐ Falls	☐ Ocean	☐ Lake
☐ Desert	☐ Mount	☐ River	☐ Sea

1. Grand _Canyon_

2. Amazon _____

3. _____ Superior

4. _____ Fuji

5. Mediterranean _____

6. Niagara _____

7. Pacific _____

8. Sahara _____

2 *Write the comparative and superlative of the words given.*

> **Spelling note: Comparatives and superlatives**
>
> | | Adjective | Comparative | Superlative |
> |---|---|---|---|
> | Add **-er** or **-est** to most words: | long | long**er** | the long**est** |
> | Add **-r** or **-st** to words ending in **-e:** | large | larg**er** | the larg**est** |
> | Drop **y** and add **-ier** or **-iest:** | dry | dr**ier** | the dr**iest** |
> | Double the final consonant and add **-er** or **-est:** | big | bigg**er** | the bigg**est** |

1. busy   *busier*   *the busiest*   6. noisy _____ _____

2. cool _____ _____   7. old _____ _____

3. friendly _____ _____   8. safe _____ _____

4. heavy _____ _____   9. small _____ _____

5. nice _____ _____   10. wet _____ _____

3 *Complete this conversation.*
Use the superlative of the words given.

The Grand Canal

Ian: So where did you go for your vacation, Val?

Val: Italy.

Ian: How exciting! Did you have a good time?

Val: It was terrific! I think Italy is

    the most exciting (exciting)

    country in Europe.

Ian: Well, it certainly has some of

    _____ (famous)

    cities in the world – Rome, Milan, Venice.

Val: Yeah. I had _____ (good) time in Venice.

    It's _____ (beautiful) city I've ever seen.

    Of course, it's also one of _____ (popular)

    tourist attractions. It was _____ (crowded)

    city I visited this summer, and there weren't even any cars!

Ian: I've always wanted to visit Venice. What's it like in the winter?

Val: Actually, that's _____ (bad) time to visit.

    Venice is one of _____ (cold and foggy)

    places in Italy in the winter.

4 *Did you know? Complete these sentences. Use the comparative or the superlative of the words given.*

The Suez Canal, Egypt

Mount Waialeale, USA

Death Valley, USA

1. Canada and Russia are _____*the largest*_____ (large) countries in the world.

2. Russia is _____*larger than*_____ (large) Canada.

3. _____ (high) waterfall in the world is in Venezuela.

4. The Suez Canal joins the Mediterranean and Red seas. It is 190 kilometers (118 miles) long. It is _____ (long) the Panama Canal.

5. The Atacama Desert in Chile is _____ (dry) place in the world.

6. Mount Waialeale in Hawaii gets 1,170 centimeters (460 inches) of rain a year. It is _____ (wet) place on earth!

7. _____ (hot) capital city in the world is Muscat, in Oman.

8. The continent of Antarctica is _____ (cold) any other place in the world.

9. The Himalayas are some of _____ (dangerous) mountains to climb.

10. Badwater, in California's Death Valley, is _____ (low) point in North America.

11. Mont Blanc in the French Alps is _____ (high) the Matterhorn in the Swiss Alps.

12. The Pacific Ocean is _____ (deep) the Atlantic Ocean. In some places the Pacific Ocean is 11,033 meters (36,198 feet) deep.

81

5 *The coldest and the windiest!*

A Where is the coldest place you've ever been?

B Read about Antarctica.

ANTARCTICA is the most southern continent in the world. It is like nowhere else on earth. It is much larger than Europe, and nearly twice the size of Australia. It is an icy plateau with the South Pole at its center. Antarctica is the coldest and windiest place in the world, even colder and windier than the North Pole. In the summer, the sun shines for twenty-four hours a day, but in the winter it's completely dark for about three months. Very few plants grow there, but there is some wildlife, including whales, seals, and penguins.

When Captain James Cook sailed around the continent in the 1770s, he found no one living there. Today, a few scientists work in Antarctica, but they only spend fairly short periods there. Many scientists in Antarctica are studying the ozone layer. The ozone layer is getting thinner and thinner worldwide. The biggest "hole" is over Antarctica, where the weather is getting warmer. Scientists think that this cold and lonely place can teach us a lot about the earth and how to keep it safe.

C Check (✓) True or False.

	True	False
1. Europe is bigger than Antarctica.	☐	☐
2. The North Pole is the coldest and windiest place in the world.	☐	☐
3. In Antarctica, it never gets dark in the summer.	☐	☐
4. There are a lot of animals and birds in Antarctica.	☐	☐
5. Captain Cook found a few scientists living in Antarctica.	☐	☐
6. The weather in Antarctica is getting colder and colder.	☐	☐

6 Geography quiz

Use the words in the box. Write questions about the pictures.
Then circle the correct answers.

☐ How big   ☐ How deep   ☐ How long
☐ How cold   ☐ How far   ☑ How high

Angel Falls (Venezuela)

1. *How high is Angel Falls?*
   a. It's 979 meters (3,212 feet) tall.
   b. It's 979 meters high. ⟵ circled

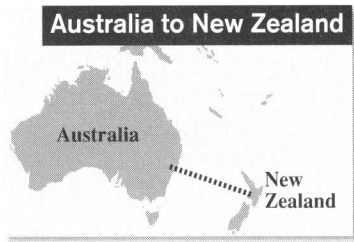
Australia to New Zealand

2. _____
   a. It's about 2,000 kilometers (12,000 miles).
   b. It's about 2,000 square kilometers.

the Amazon River

3. _____
   a. It's 6,437 kilometers (4,000 miles) long.
   b. It's 6,437 kilometers high.

Antarctica

4. _____
   a. It gets up to −88.3 degrees Celsius
      (−126.9 degrees Fahrenheit).
   b. It gets down to −88.3 degrees Celsius.

the Amazon Rain Forest

5. _____
   a. It's 6 million square kilometers (2½ million miles).
   b. It's 6 million kilometers long.

the Grand Canyon

6. _____
   a. It's about 1.6 kilometers (1 mile) big.
   b. It's about 1.6 kilometers deep.

7 *Write the opposites.*

Across

2 biggest
6 bad
7 shorter
8 worse
9 worst
10 near
11 lowest
13 driest
14 hot
15 shortest

Down

1 hotter
3 smaller
4 least crowded (2 words)
5 coldest
9 smallest
10 not famous
11 cold
12 best

15 I'm going to see a musical.

1

Which nouns often go with which verbs? Complete the chart. Use each word only once.

- ☐ an amusement park
- ☑ a beach party
- ☐ a ballgame on TV
- ☐ a barbecue
- ☐ a museum
- ☐ a play
- ☐ a rock concert
- ☐ a video

have	see	visit	watch
a beach party			

2

Read Anna's diary, and write about her plans. Use the present continuous.

July

Sunday	Monday	Tuesday	Wednesday	Thursday	Friday	Saturday
6 morning – visit Forest Green Historic Park	**7** work overtime to finish the report	**8** 7:00 P.M. see a play with Tony	**9** night – watch the hockey game with Kate & Sam	**10** 12:00 noon have a barbecue	**11** stay home and watch the late show on TV	**12** afternoon – go to an arts festival

1. On Sunday morning, Anna is visiting Forest Green Historic Park.

2. _____

3. _____

4. _____

5. _____

6. _____

7. _____

85

3 *Complete this conversation. Use* **be going to** *and the verbs given.*

Marta: What ___are___ you ___going to do___ this weekend, Mark?   (do)

Mark: I _____ to an art gallery on Saturday.   (go)

Marta: That sounds interesting.

Mark: Yeah. There's a new exhibit at the Modern. And how about you, Marta?

Marta: Well, Brian and I _____ a ballgame
in the afternoon.   (see)

Mark: And what _____ you _____ in the evening?   (do)

Marta: Brian _____ his mother in the hospital.   (visit)

But I _____ not _____ anything really.   (do)

Mark: Well, I _____ some friends over

for a barbecue. Would you like to come?   (have)

Marta: Thanks. I'd love to.

4 *Choose the correct responses.*

1. A: Would you like to go to a movie on Sunday?

   B: *Oh, I'm sorry. I can't.* _____
   - Oh, I'm sorry. I can't.
   - Nothing special.
   - No. I wouldn't.

2. A: Do you want to visit the street fair with us tomorrow?

   B: _____
   - Yes, I'm going to.
   - Can we go to a late show?
   - Sure, I'd love to.

3. A: We're having friends over for dinner tonight. Would you like to come?

   B: _____
   - How about this evening?
   - I'm working late tonight. I'm sorry.
   - Yes, it would.

4. A: How about dinner at the Mexican restaurant tonight?

   B: _____
   - No, I'm not doing anything.
   - Sorry, I'm going away next week.
   - Great! But it's my turn to pay.

5 *Write invitations to this week's events in Princeville.*

Exciting things to do this week in **Princeville**   All events scheduled to begin at 8:00 P.M.

Wednesday	Thursday	Friday	Saturday
Rock concert The Cranberries	**Amusement park** Lots to do for everyone!	**Play** *Funny Money*	**Museum** Exhibition of modern art

1. *Are you doing anything on Wednesday evening? Do you want to see a rock concert?*
   or *I'm going to see the Cranberries on Wednesday. Would you like to come?*

2. _____

   _____

3. _____

   _____

4. _____

   _____

6 *Write about how often you do these leisure activities.*
Use the expressions in the box.

I often . . . . I . . . almost every weekend. I sometimes . . . in the summer. I . . . three or four times a year. I never . . . .

1. *I never go to rock concerts.*

2. _____

3. _____

4. _____

5. _____

6. _____

1. go to rock concerts
2. go for long walks
3. have parties at home
4. see plays
5. visit amusement parks
6. watch ballgames

87

7 *Beyond the telephone*

A Why do you use the telephone? List some reasons.

_____

_____

B Read the passage. Are the reasons different from the ones in your list?

TODAY'S TELEPHONES

www.telephone.com

Not so long ago, people only used the telephone to make phone calls. Now, thanks to computers, people use their phones to do much more. They can bank by phone, rent videos by phone, and even shop by phone. It is also possible to send letters and reports by faxing them over telephone lines. People can even use their phone lines to send messages from one computer to another computer by electronic mail, or *e-mail*.

But you don't need to be at home or at the office to use the phone anymore. You can carry a cellular phone in your pocket or keep one in your car. With a cellular phone, anyone who can talk and walk can also *phone* and walk. You don't have to look for a pay phone to make a call anymore. Now you can take your calls with you everywhere.

C Check (✓) True or False. For statements that are false, write the true information.

	True	False
1. You can pay for things by phone.	☐	☐
2. Fax machines do not use telephone lines.	☐	☐
3. You need a computer and a telephone line to send e-mail.	☐	☐
4. You can use a cellular phone at home or at work.	☐	☐
5. You need a car to make a call on a cellular phone.	☐	☐

8 *Read these messages. What did the caller say?*
Write the messages another way using **tell** *or* **ask.**

For:	Ms. Tam
Message:	*The meeting is at 10:30 tomorrow morning.* *Bring the last fax from New York.*

1. <u>Please tell Ms. Tam that the meeting is at 10:30 tomorrow morning. . . .</u>

_____

For:	Mr. Alvarez
Message:	*We need the report by noon. Call Ms. James as soon as possible.*

2. _____

_____

For:	Dr. James
Message:	*The new fax machine is ready. Pick it up this afternoon.*

3. _____

_____

9 *Look at the message slips. Ask someone to give these messages.*

Grammar note: Negative infinitives	
Request	**Message**
Don't call him today.	Please ask Jan **not to call** him today.
Don't go home yet.	Could you tell him **not to go** home yet?

Michael -
Don't meet me at the airport
until midnight. The plane is
going to be late.

1. _____

_____

_____

Lucy —
We're meeting at Dino's house before
the concert. Don't forget the tickets.

2. _____

_____

Christopher —
The beach party starts at noon.
Don't be late!

3. _____

_____

10 Choose the correct words.

Secretary: Hello. Grant and Lee.

Ms. Curtis: _May I_ speak to Ms. Grace Schmidt, please?
(May I/Would you)

Secretary: I'm _____ . She's not in. _____
(busy/sorry)   (Can I leave/Can I take)
a message?

Ms. Curtis: Yes, please. This is Ms. Curtis. _____ you
(Would/Please)

_____ I'm staying at the Plaza Hotel?
(tell her that/ask her to)

The number is 735-9001, Room 605. _____
(Please/Could)

you _____ ?
(tell her to call me/tell her to call her)

Secretary: OK, Ms. Curtis. I'll _____ the message.
(give her/tell her)

Ms. Curtis: Thank you very much. Good-bye.

11 Match the questions with the correct responses.

☐ Yes, please. Could you tell him Ros called? ☐ Let me see if he's in.
☐ That's OK. I'll call back. ☐ My name's Graham. Graham Lock.
☐ Yes. My number is 669-3241. ☑ Yes, that would be great. Thanks.

1. Would you like to come to a party?
Yes, that would be great. Thanks.

2. Could I ask her to call you back?
_____

3. Who's calling?
_____

4. Can I take a message?
_____

5. Could I speak to Paul, please?
_____

6. I'm sorry. She's busy at the moment.
_____

16 A change for the better!

1 Choose the correct responses.

1. A: Say, you really look different.

   B: _Well, my hair is a little longer now._
      - I moved into a new house.
      - I'm more outgoing now.
      - Well, my hair is a little longer now.

2. A: I haven't seen you for ages.

   B: _____
      - I know. How have you been?
      - Well, I quit smoking.
      - My new job is more stressful.

3. A: You know, I have three kids now.

   B: _____
      - Well, I've grown a mustache.
      - That's terrific!
      - Say, you've really changed your hair.

4. A: How are you?

   B: _____
      - I do more aerobics these days.
      - Well, actually, I have contact lenses now.
      - I'm doing really well.

2 Complete the sentences. Use information in the box and the present perfect.

- ☑ move to a new apartment
- ☐ spend a lot of money on clothes
- ☐ start going to the gym
- ☐ stop eating out in restaurants

1. Judy _'s moved to a new apartment_ .
   Her old one was too small.

2. Kim and Anna _____ .
   Now they cook dinner at home every evening. It's much cheaper.

3. Alex _____ .
   He looks healthier, and he has more energy.

4. Jerry _____ .
   He needs to dress up for his new job.

3 *Describe how these people have changed.*
Use the present or the past tense.

1. *Shawn lost a lot of weight.*

2. _____

3. _____

4 *Rewrite these sentences. Find another way to say each*
sentence using the words given.

1. Alice quit eating rich food.
   Alice eats healthier foods now. _____ (healthier)

2. James lost a lot of weight.
   _____ (heavier)

3. Mary goes to a new school now.
   _____ (change)

4. Tess isn't married anymore.
   _____ (divorce)

5. I've grown my hair.
   _____ (longer)

6. We don't smoke anymore.
   _____ (quit)

5 Life changes

A *Have you ever . . .*

☐ lost a job
☐ had money problems
☐ had trouble making friends
☐ worked in a foreign country

B Read the passages on the left. Then read the passages on the right. Match the people's lives two years ago with their lives today. Underline at least two changes in each person's life.

Aki

Luis and his wife

Rosie

Two years ago	Now
1. Aki Two years ago, I was a student, and I thought life was really good. I got up late. I spent the day talking to friends, and then I studied all night. I wore jeans and sweatshirts and had long hair and a mustache. I felt free. _____	**a.** Now my life has changed. I got married! My wife and I often have friends over for dinner. We're taking evening classes. It's great!
2. Luis I moved to a new town two years ago. My job was interesting, but I was single, and I didn't have any friends. People at work were friendly but not very outgoing. We never did anything after work. _____	**b.** Now I work as a computer programmer for an international company. I've moved to Seoul and have started to learn Korean. Korean food is great, and I've gained several kilos. I feel much happier and healthier.
3. Rosie My life seemed to come to an end two years ago. I lost my job. Then I lost weight, and looked terrible. Money became a problem. I was very sad. I needed some good luck. _____	**c.** Now I actually look forward to getting up early in the morning and going to work. Of course, I dress up now, and my hair is shorter. But I don't really mind. At least my evenings are free!

6 *Complete the sentences. Use words in the box.*

☐ broke	☑ graduation	☐ loan	☐ retire	☐ successful	☐ responsible

1. After _____ *graduation* _____ , I plan to look for a job.

2. Marie lost her job. Now she's _____ , and she can't pay her rent.

3. Now that I'm going to college, I want to be more _____ about doing my classwork.

4. Lucy wants to pay off her student _____ before she buys a car.

5. Philip plans to _____ at an early age. He's almost 55 now.

6. I'd like to be _____ in my first job. Then I can get a better job and a raise.

7 *Complete this conversation. Use the words given.*

Melissa: What _____ *do you plan to do* _____ (plan, do) this summer, Leo?

Leo: I _____ (want, get) a summer job.

I _____ (like, save) money for a vacation.

Melissa: Really? Where _____ (like, go) ?

Leo: Well, I _____ (love, travel) to Latin America. What about you, Melissa?

Melissa: I _____ (not go, get) a job right away.

I _____ (want, go) to Spain and Portugal.

Leo: Sounds great, but how _____ (go, pay) for it?

Melissa: I _____ (hope, borrow) some money from my brother. I have a good excuse. I

_____ (plan, take) courses in Spanish and Portuguese.

Leo: Oh, I'm tired of studying!

Melissa: So am I. But I also _____ (hope, take) people on tours to Latin America. Why don't you come on my first tour?

8 *Imagine you have these problems. Write three sentences about changing these situations. Use words in the box.*

1. I'm not interested in my job these days. I spend three hours driving to and from work every day, and I don't make enough money! I can't find a new job, though, because of my poor computer skills.

| I hope to . . . . | I want to . . . . | I plan to . . . . |

_____

_____

_____

2. I've become less careful about my health lately. I've stopped jogging because I'm bored with it. I've started smoking because I have terrible problems at work. And I'm always tired because I can't sleep at night.

| I'm going to . . . . | I'd like to . . . . | I'd love to . . . . |

_____

_____

_____

3. I just moved to a new town, and I don't know anyone. People at work are friendly but not very outgoing – I never do anything after work. I haven't had a date in about four months. And I live outside of town, so I don't have many neighbors.

| I'm going to . . . . | I want to . . . . | I plan to . . . . |

_____

_____

_____

4

9   *Choose the correct words to complete each sentence. Use the correct form of the word or add any words necessary.*

1. William would like   <u>   *to retire*   </u>   early – around 50.   (retire / marry / divorce)

2. Heather's salary is much <u>   </u> before. She had to take a pay cut.   (low / short / high)

3. I dress up for my new job, and I'm always on time now. I'm <u>   </u> these days.   (different / outgoing / responsible)

4. After graduation, Jack plans <u>   </u> for an international company.   (retire / work / move)

5. This job is <u>   </u> my last job. (responsible / stressful / expensive)

6. Mel hopes <u>   </u> to a small town. (move / live / change)

---

10   *Advise people how to make changes in their lives. Use expressions like the ones in the box.*

> You should . . . .
> You shouldn't . . . .
> Why don't you . . . ?

1. I've gained a lot of weight this year.
   <u>*You should be more careful about your diet.*</u>
   or <u>*Why don't you spend more time at the gym?*</u>

2. My hair is longer, but it doesn't look good.
   _____

3. I've gotten tired of wearing the same old clothes.
   _____

4. I want to start a successful business.
   _____

5. I'm often bored on weekends.
   _____

6. The food I cook always tastes bland.
   _____

7. I hope to retire early.
   _____

8. I've finished *New Interchange Book 1,* but I still want to improve my English!
   _____